This Meal We Share

An additional text
for Holy Communion

Graham Jeffery

Kevin
Mayhew

First published in 1998 by
KEVIN MAYHEW LTD
Rattlesden
Bury St Edmunds
Suffolk IP30 0SZ

© 1998 Graham Jeffery

0 1 2 3 4 5 6 7 8 9

ISBN 1 84003 008 9
Catalogue No 1500112

Front cover photography:
Bread and chalice by Bruce Head
Stained glass window reflection by Derek Forss

Front cover photo composition and design by Jaquetta Sergeant
Typesetting by Louise Selfe
Printed and bound in Great Britain by
Caligraving Limited Thetford Norfolk

Contents

Have we not started again from the beginning with the liturgy . . . even if 'starting from the beginning' is only an illusion, because in reality things continue, because in the church which is a living body and a living reality, everything is continuous.

CARLO CARETTO
Blessed are you who believed

Preface

If only there were no reason for this book to exist!

This is not the kind of remark that will endear me to publishers, but they need have no fear because there are all too many reasons for this book to exist.

Let me clarify what I mean. When churches come to choose candidates for ordination, I wonder how high a priority they give to the candidates' capacity to lead people in prayer, their natural competence in presiding at liturgies, speaking with ease, competence and dignity from among and on behalf of the community, to be able to speak from the heart and not simply out of a book, and yet at the same time to speak with authority and conviction in the name of the Church.

Impossible? The early Church clearly did not think so, as witness the evidence:

- from Justin's *Apology* (Justin was martyred around AD 165) which describes how Christians gather on a Sunday for the prayer of thanksgiving which is pronounced by 'the one who presides for as long as he is able . . .' [1, 67];

- from the *Didaché* (dated sometime between AD 80 and 130) which speaks of celebrants giving thanks 'as much as they wish' [X, 7];

- from the document we know as the *Apostolic Tradition*, and which describes liturgical practice in early-third-century Rome: having given an example of a eucharistic prayer, Hippolytus adds explicitly, 'The bishop does not have to pronounce exactly the words given here . . . rather, each prays as best he can . . .'.

Of course, as time went past, people noted down the best of what they heard good celebrants saying and adapted it to their own communities. This, for example, is how we come to have three different versions of the eucharistic prayer attributed to Saint James.

As Christian theology became more sophisticated, so the

celebrant had to be careful how he prayed aloud – for the Church has always understood that how we pray betrays how we really think. So it is when the Trinity is under threat from certain heresies that Saint Basil found it only natural to make the eucharistic prayer a glorious hymn of praise of the Trinity, even so far as to invite us to sing the 'Holy, holy, holy' as a way of prayerfully affirming our Trinitarian faith.

There is no exact moment when extemporary prayer was replaced by fixed formulae, which is what the word 'Canon' means (moreover, it would be wrong to understand 'extemporary' as meaning 'spontaneous' or 'unprepared'). Certainly, the institutionalisation of the Church under Constantine played a major role in the 'bureaucratisation' of her ministries. Many years later, another Emperor, Charlemagne, was only too aware of how religion could serve as a unifying factor, and deliberately imposed what he thought was the best model then available, namely that of papal liturgy in Rome. Once the Church is modelled on the civil service, of course things are done 'by the book'.

There is a sense in which the force of the liturgical reform in this century has been to acknowledge that we do things 'by the book' and therefore try and make sure 'the book' is as good as possible. And there is no doubting that the official liturgical books we now have, intelligently used, provide the primary source for good liturgy. Indeed, at various points the rubrics in the official books specifically invite the celebrant to pray 'in these or in similar words'. However – and prudently, I would acknowledge – very little latitude is offered (as yet?) in the eucharistic prayers.

However, it still remains true that all good liturgy must be faithful, not only to the tradition of the Church, but also must be faithful to those who gather to celebrate. This is where the true genius of bishops of the early Church lay: speaking the language of their own community, and gathering up their concerns, their joys and sorrows, they could express this in a way which lifted the people's hearts through Christ in the Spirit to the Father. They were true both to the Church in its most universal sense of transcending space and time, and also to that very real sacrament of the universal Church which was their own local community.

Too few though they may be, there are among us today poet priests, deeply sensitive people, who, while doing what the Church has always done, have the gift of being able to express this undying tradition in the words which they know best suit the assembly gathered in that particular place on that particular day.

This Meal We Share is a collection of such prayers, by one such individual. I know his genuine humility will make him cringe at the praise which is explicit in my words; but his is not the false humility that would make him hide or even renounce this God-given talent. Let us honour his skill and respect his humility by accepting this collection in the spirit in which he offers it.

The best service this book can possibly render is that it be imitated rather than simply used. If this becomes nothing but a book of prayers to replace another book of prayers, then it will have failed – especially if it is used instead of the official prayers of the liturgy.

Rather, this collection shows how, nourished on the prayers of the official liturgy, a good celebrant can make these come alive. Sometimes, it may be simply by an intelligent delivery, praying from the heart – albeit with words from a book. Sometimes – as most good priests know from experience – it may be slipping in an extra word or two.

This is what this collection represents: those extra couple of words by a profoundly pastoral poet. May his attempts, humbly offered, encourage you as you pray with and in the name of your community.

ROBERT KELLY
Liturgy Consultant

Introduction

We all find security in the landmarks of our church's prayers and liturgies, made familiar from childhood or becoming so: keeping us company and binding our lives and communities together. The aim of this collection of prayers is to offer little helps to go around the bread and wine, for those perhaps unused to formal liturgies, and for those to whom the established words may have become a barrier to worship. Where this is the case, one or two of the prayers in each section can be used to assist the established version.

It is my hope and prayer that, through these prayers, others may be helped to find their own landmarks in him who is our only rock: and by whose spirit the most inadequate of prayers are made into love.

There are three elements in the meeting of God's people to celebrate the Eucharist.

The *reading of the Gospel* and, if God permits, the preaching in which the good news of God's love and his plan for each one of us is told again and proclaimed to his people. Proclamation is not the same as turning up the volume of a broadcast. It is the telling again of perhaps obvious truths in so compassionate and urgent a way that people are able to believe more passionately themselves what they knew perfectly well before the service started.

The second element in worship is *the blessing of the bread and wine* in a meal to which everyone is invited, and around a table at which everyone has a place. The life and death of Jesus of Nazareth is shown forth in this breaking until he comes again – though in fact the communion is a way of making him come again: helping him do so, though he is already here. The offering of the bread and wine is the offering of our own lives also. To give light where we experience darkness: to return love, by God's grace, when we receive only neglect or perhaps hatred.

The third element in Christian worship is *the prayer and the preparation of the people* beforehand. An act of worship may be for some of the congregation the first time they have been to church. So they will have had no time for conscious preparation. But the celebrant is part of that living community which meets and is made a community by that meeting. He or she needs to 'collect' the wishes of the people before they can be gathered together and offered as a Collect. The prayers offered need not be long or in any particular order. They can be offered as appropriately by means of a welcome to particular people, or 'asides' between hymns or readings concerning people's anniversaries or needs, or sickness or return to health. The celebrant may not even preach as such. But it is crucial that he or she knows the congregation by name, so far as is possible, and is their listener and their friend.

The celebrant who spends seven minutes in prayer or speaking in a service has always spent seven hours listening to his people, or to God in them, beforehand. Most of the iceberg is under the water and no 'public' worship can be sustained 'above the water' unless a far deeper mass of love and care and apparently doing nothing is there underneath to hold it up.

There are such things as 'visiting' preachers and celebrants, as there are occasions when the father or mother of a family asks an honoured friend to carve or serve the Sunday joint. But no child expects their food to be given at the hand of strangers. No more do we. God's word and food is given to us by those who have laboured to provide it – who love us, live for us, and wish us well.

The good celebrant, like the good shepherd, gives his life for the sheep.

It is not where you lived then
    that matters, Lord.
In that place,
    or that people,
    or that liturgy.
But where you live now,
    in these servants,
    waiting to be fed,
    this people, waiting to be healed
    and lifted high,
    waiting to be nourished
    and refreshed,
    to serve you to your glory.

GRAHAM JEFFERY

The Gathering of God's People

Go into the village, and a man will meet you, carrying a pitcher of water . . . He will show you a large room upstairs, set out in readiness . . .
Mark 14:13-15

No service or celebration of holy communion can start without someone, a man in this instance doing the job normally reserved for women, showing himself to be a servant in his care for others, without thought for his own position.

The priest or celebrant's care for his people the week before, knowing them by name, tending to their humblest need, is not an optional extra before the celebration of the Lord's supper. It is a crucial prelude to it.

Those who come to the Lord's supper are cherished, prayed for and welcomed. 'Come to me, all who travail and are heavy laden, and I will refresh you.' Not just at the service itself, but the week before, and the week after.

Celebrant We will come into your house, Lord.

People We are your house,
    we are the household of your faith.

Celebrant We will come into your presence, Lord.

People We are in your presence daily,
    we love you, we serve you,
    we give you praise.

Celebrant We will meet around your table, Lord.

People Your table is our table,
    your bread and wine,
    our own flesh and blood.
Dear Lord, we praise you daily.

1   Our souls wait for you, Lord.
    It is you who call us to this day,
        and to each other's company.
    We wait for your Spirit, Lord.
    Only then can we think.
    We wait for your word in our hearts,
        only then can we listen,
        only then can we proclaim.
    Come to us, Lord.
    Come to us quickly.
    Make yourself known to us
        in the bread's breaking.

2   Come to us, Lord,
        in the power of your Spirit.
    We do not know what to say
        until you tell us how to think,
        unless you help us to live,
        unless you assist us.
    Come to us, Lord.
    Come to us now.
    In the power of your Son Jesus,
        we praise your name.

3   Where two or three are gathered
        in love's name, for love's purpose,
        to listen, not to speak,
        to wait on the Lord,
        not tell him what to do:
        then God is present,
        love is present,
        and Jesus of Nazareth rises again
        from the tomb.

4   So many blessed by so obscure a life.
    So many fed by one who hungers for our love.
    So many lifted high
       by one who was himself abased.
    So many comforted
       by one who died in loneliness.
    Dear Lord,
       I do not need to lift my heart to you,
       but ask you to come down,
       here where you are already.

5   We brought nothing into this world, Lord.
    We bring nothing into this house,
       this meeting of your people,
       except our needs and emptiness,
       waiting to be filled.
    We brought nothing into this place.
    Fill us now, Lord, with your Spirit.
    Make us your people once again.

6   The table is prepared, Lord.
    Your table, your feast,
       your love invites us all.
    In the company of saints and angels,
       we your people love you.
    Share with each other
       the life of your Son Jesus,
       made possible for us by your Spirit.
    We proclaim him.
    We set forth our own faith in his life.
    We give you glory.

7   One thing we ask of you, Lord,
           to dwell in your house,
           in your people,
           in the life of your Son.
       We come before you with praises,
           but also with needs,
           and emptiness waiting to be filled.
       We wait on your word, Lord.
       It directs us and comforts us,
           it feeds us
           and nourishes our souls.
       We sing to your glory.

8   You visit the earth, Lord.
       Daily in this sacrament
           your word is made flesh
           and dwells among us.
       This people gathered,
           this meal prepared,
           this life set forth
           and proclaimed once again.
       We meet in your Spirit, Lord,
           and await your guiding.

9   Dear Lord, your table is ready.
       Our chairs set in order,
           each one of us has our proper place
           in your kingdom.
       The bread and wine are prepared,
           sacraments of your great love for us.
       You provide for us daily.
       The gospels are open,
           that you may speak to us again,
           and we with you.

10   What has been believed,
        by all peoples in all places at all times.
     This we proclaim.
     This is our faith.
     This is our only life.
     What has been believed by one person,
        at one time, in one place.
     Jesus on his cross,
        loving us to the end.
     This is our faith.
     This is our only life.

11   We are your people, Lord.
     Your holy community.
     It is this only
        according to your grace,
           that makes possible this sacrament of union.
     With your whole Church,
        we give you glory.
     The living and the departed praise you,
        in union with your Son.

12   It is not where we are that defines us, Lord,
        it is where we shall be.
     Not who we are, or what we have done,
        but who is at work within us,
        who loves us,
        who leads us.
     We meet in your Son's name, Lord,
        but also in our own.
     It is you who call us,
        and give us our meaning.

13   Where two or three meet in your name, Lord,
                      you are there.
                Your whole Church is there.
                We do not come to you on our own.
                We follow the apostles*

                *Make mention here of saints connected with the local church, the current feast day, or the patron of the people with whom you are celebrating.

14   We believe in you, Lord,
                      but also in ourselves.
                Our own calling
                      by the sea of Galilee,
                      our own hearing
                      of your word to us.
                We come to you, Lord.
                We follow.
                Not in our own goodness trusting,
                      but in your great love,
                      we approach
                      this holy table.

15   We believe in you, Lord,
                      but also in ourselves.
                We are your community,
                      your people, waiting to be fed.
                Your people, waiting to be led
                      by your word of loving kindness
                      for all of us,
                      for each one of us.
                Even so, Lord Jesus,
                      come quickly.

Waiting on the Holy Scripture

Did we not feel our hearts on fire as he spoke with us . . . ?
Luke 24:32

The first two disciples to hear an Easter sermon from Jesus in person contributed to the sermon as much as he did. As we do. For while the preacher commends the gospel as well as he may, he is a listener also. Seeking to preach to that human condition he has been bearing and listening to all week.

The preacher listens to the word of Jesus more than others do. For he has to preach to himself on Sundays, as well as console and strengthen other people. He can do nothing without the prayers and support of his congregation. Their contribution is always paramount. There are no great preachers, only great congregations.

1   Lead us in your way, Lord.
Your word to us is truth.
Lead us in your paths.
Your life is our only guide.
Help us to follow you, Lord,
    even when we cannot see your footsteps.
Your word leads us in our lives now.

2   We wait for you to act, Lord,
    never ourselves.
For you to lead us by your star.
We will follow your star, Lord,
    not our own wishes.
Not certain where it leads,
    we travel onward.

3   Our time is in your hand, Lord,
      in this moment we are still.
Not for you to speak,
      but for you to love.
You love us always,
      care for us, redeem us.
Lift us up, Lord,
      help us to hear the sound of your silences
      and the waves on Galilee's beach.
Your silence is louder, Lord,
      than the world's noise and speaking.
In your silence you come to us,
      and lift us high.

4   I listen to your word, Lord.
May your wine and oil
      increase in our hearts.
Wine to make glad our hearts,
      oil to be poured
      in our deepest wounds,
      our most tender neglects.
Lord, come to us quickly.

5   Your life speaks to us, Lord,
      louder than words,
      but not louder than
      the word of life
      held in our hearts.
Help us to listen to your word,
      and hold it safe.
Help us to see with our eyes,
      to hear with our ears
      and in our hearts,
      to walk, in your way
      not only with our feet,
      but in our lives.

6   Why do you stand so far off, Lord,
       hiding your face
       when we most need to see you?
     Come to us now, Lord.
     Show us the light of your countenance,
       your peace.
     Lord, speak to us,
       your people are waiting.

7   We build our altars in one place, Lord.
     These hearts ready,
       these lives dedicated to your word.
     This people present.
     This sacrament prepared.
     This message of comfort,
       waiting to be given.
     We build our altars in one place, Lord.
     Send down your fire upon us,
       as you will:
       wherever you will.

8   Your Church has made many mistakes, Lord.
     Help her not to add to them
       by making the last mistake of all,
       and ceasing to exist.
     Help us to cling to your word, Lord.
     Help us to cling to each other.
     Help us to build
       on your foundations only.

The Confession

During supper, Jesus . . . took a towel and tied it round him. Then he poured water into a basin and began to wash his disciples' feet . . .
John 13:3-5

In the confession we expose the most vulnerable parts of our life to God's love. Those parts of us which touch the ground and get most muddy. We confess our sins and failures with each other, and to each other. But what we are really 'confessing' is God's merciful love! Though the celebrant says the words of absolution, it is God who declares them, washing away all that hinders our walk with God and enabling us to start again.

Of course, being human is a very messy business. And the apostles were not saints, at least until they were dead. But the fact we are bound to get our feet muddy on Monday is no barrier to washing them the day before, and every day.

May the Lord absolve and bless all his sinners, 'of whom I am the chief' (St Paul, 1 Timothy 1:15).

1   This world is for forgiving other people, Lord,
    when they hurt us,
    when they neglect us.
Eternity is for forgiving ourselves,
    knowing that we are this moment
    and every moment totally loved,
    totally understood,
    totally forgiven.
We bring our own sins before you, Lord.
You know what they are, who we are.
You stretch out your hand toward us,
    and we are healed.

2

We are not worthy, Lord,
   to approach your table.
And yet we are worthy,
   your Spirit makes us so,
   your love poured into our hearts.
We confess our sins, Lord,
   those ways not taken.
That way of love and sacrifice
   not followed.
We confess to you our sins.
But we confess our faith also.
Your love for us above all,
   comforts us, refreshes us,
   renews us, heals us.
Lord, I am not worthy.
But you are.

3

Inside every sinner, Lord,
   there is a saint waiting to get out.
Inside every broken soul,
   a mended spirit waiting to be whole.
In our lives also,
   you are always with us.
No besetting sin can keep you away.
You who are our friend always.

4

We confess our sins, Lord,
   to you and before each other.
The things we have left undone.
The things done wrongly.
Paths not taken.
The path turned away from.
You never leave us, Lord,
   however far we stray.
Your love calls us back.
We confess our sins to you,
   who love us and are with us always.

5   Forgive us our sins, Lord,
    those things we have done wrongly,
    those good things we have not done,
    that good path we have not taken.
   Help us to do better, Lord,
    in our trusting of you
    to help us and redeem us.
   May our hearts and minds be filled
    with your goodness,
    not our own weakness.
   Come to us, Lord, now, today.
   When we are lowly in our own eyes,
    you lift us up.

6   We kneel before you, Lord.
   Not what we are now,
    but what we shall be.
   Not where we are now,
    but where your Spirit will lead us.
   We kneel with your Son Jesus
    before the possibilities
    of our own lives also.

7   We confess our sins, Lord,
    but also our virtues.
   Those things we have done well,
    those good things we tried to be,
    even if we failed.
   We confess our faith, Lord,
    before each other
    and in our own hearts,
    that you come to us as a people,
    but also one by one.
   You bless us, sustain us, forgive us.
   Give us your peace.

8　　We confess our sins to you, Lord,
　　　　but also to each other.
　　The state of the world is our fault.
　　We are all to blame,
　　　　but only partly to blame.
　　Our sins and our virtues are inherited in part.
　　We influence each other for good or evil.
　　Help our prayer for each other.
　　We bring you our sins, Lord,
　　　　of thought, word and deed.
　　Our lives are open to you.
　　We await your blessing.

9　　Be merciful to our sins, Lord,
　　　　for they are great.
　　But your love for us is greater.
　　Speedily you come to us,
　　　　stop your donkey on the road
　　　　where we have fallen,
　　　　pour in your own oil and wine
　　　　carry us to your inn,
　　　　help us to continue our journey.
　　You are our journey, Lord,
　　　　but also our companion on the way.

10　　On the night of your betrayal, Lord,
　　　　your gave us your own self,
　　　　your own Spirit,
　　　　though we betray you
　　　　and do not understand.
　　Through our betrayal, you come to us.
　　Give us your love
　　　　the bread your hand has broken,
　　　　the wine your life has blessed.
　　We receive you, Lord,
　　　　the forgiveness of your love.
　　Your Spirit comes to us.

The Pharisees brought in a woman detected in the very act of adultery . . . Making her stand out in the middle they said to him, 'In the law Moses laid down that such women are to be stoned. What do you say about it?' . . . Jesus bent down and wrote with his finger on the ground.
John 7:53

11   Write in the sand again, Lord.
Do not let the world draw attention
    to our misdeeds.
Draw the attention of the world
    to what we wanted to be,
    not what we are.
And when the crowds are gone
    and we are alone,
    you and ourselves together,
    lift up your hands to bless us.
Sending us out to serve you,
    to the Father's glory.

12   You so love the world, Lord,
    your servants, each one of us,
    you so love your people,
    that you give us your own Son,
    to be our friend,
    to die for us daily,
    to bring us life.
Come to us now.
Father send your Spirit,
    make clean our hearts
    to love you and hear you.
We confess our sins which so trouble us
    so burden us, hinder our race
    in running the way of your command.

13

Our sins of thought, we humbly confess.
Of cowardice, of boldness without thought.
We confess our sins,
    of things done or said
    against your word.
Of things not done or said
    to assist your kingdom.
We confess our faith, our trust in you,
    who absolve us.
Embrace us, cherish us,
    and never condemn.
Now and in eternity.

14

We bring before you our sins, Lord,
    but also our virtues.
Those graces and gifts
    your love has given us.
Opportunities to serve you,
    help us to use them wisely.
Opportunities to love you
    in the brothers and sisters
    your love affords us today.

We confess our sins to God but also our faith.
If our heart condemns us,
God is greater than our heart and knows all things.

A FORM OF CONFESSION

All

For all my sins, dear Father,
    I ask you to forgive me.
Give me your grace to sin no more,
    and in your power to live.

THE ABSOLUTION

Celebrant Grant, O Lord, to your faithful people
 pardon and peace,
 that they may be cleansed
 from all their sins
 and serve you
 with a quiet mind.
The Lord himself doth
 put away all our offences
 and gives us the grace and comfort
 of his Holy Spirit,
 in the name of the Father
 and of the Son
 and of the Holy Ghost.
 Amen.

The Preparation of the Bread and Wine

James and John approached him . . . 'Grant us to sit in state with you, one on your right hand and the other on your left.' Jesus said to them, 'You do not understand what you are asking. Can you drink the cup that I drink?'
From Mark 10:35-39

None of us can really sit at Jesus' right hand or his left. That was reserved for the two robbers who died on Good Friday, and Jesus took his place between them. So that when they looked at each other they saw each other through his eyes. He provided hope at the end.

In the same way none of us can drink Jesus' cup. Or be baptised with his own particular experience. His life was his alone, as ours is ours alone. And yet we do share his cup and drink from his life. He lives in us by the Spirit, in our own particular way.

1   You turn our water into wine, Lord.
       Our lives are not ordinary
          to you who made us.
       Hour by hour, day by day,
          all our life long
          you pass your hand over
          our ordinary lives.
       And we are ordinary no longer.
       We are your wine, Lord,
          fruit of your vineyard.
       You are the vine,
          and we are the branches.
       Day by day,
          you tend us and nourish us.

2

Bread and wine, unite us to each other.
Make us one family
  for the world's healing,
  our own redemption.
Bread and wine, link us to Jesus,
  unite us to him first of all.
For whoever finds true love is alive.
Whoever finds love,
  is united to the whole world.

3

It does not yet appear, Lord,
  what we shall be.
Your love sees what we are now,
  but also what we shall become
  by your star's leading.
Shine on us, Lord.
Shine through us,
  to your heart's content.
Save us.
Bless your people.
Save all your children.
Save the world.

4

We will sing of your love, Lord,
  for all your children.
Living and departed,
  all souls in the world's history,
  here in this moment of time.
We offer our prayers to you,
  our lives to you for the sake of others,
  that your kingdom may come in us.
With bread and wine,
  we set forth the life of your Son Jesus.

5   Our cup overflows, Lord,
         with the opportunity your love offers.
     We bring the bread of life,
         of work and celebration,
         of sorrow and of joy.
     You come to us in this feast,
         this recollection of your love for us,
         your rescuing of us in all dangers.
     Come to us now, Lord,
         come to us again,
         never leave us.
     Come to us now in the life of your Son.

6   We gather round your table, Lord.
     We are your people,
         your community,
         made so by your Spirit.
     We offer you ourselves,
         but ourselves as you see us,
         and not as the world does.
     Do not look on our sins, Lord,
         but look on our faith.
     Brothers and sisters of your Son Jesus,
         we meet in his name.
     We offer our lives to you in him.

7   The table is laid, Lord.
     Your table.
     This bread, made by our hands.
     This wine, symbol of our life,
         and of our nationhood.
     Members of your family,
         each one of us a branch on your vine,
         giving forth fruit.
     Come to us, Lord.
     Prune our minds of all unclear thoughts,
         help us to give you glory.

8   The table is set, Lord.
     Your people are gathered.
     Each one in our own place
        around your table.
     Each one having our own place
        in your kingdom.
     And yet there are more here
        than we can see or greet.
     Our friends who have died
        worship you in glory.
     We pray with them and they with us.

9   We recall your Son's birth, Lord,
        but also our own.
     We recall his death,
        show forth his love again.
     To the world, he is dead.
     His life in vain,
        his words of forgiveness have no meaning.
     But to us they are life.
     The chance to start again.
     To us he is alive for ever.

10   Your whole people praise you, Lord.
     Young and old,
        rich and poor,
        one with another.
     We are all rich in your word, Lord.
     In your estimation of us,
        of our calling.
     We meet each other around your table.
     We meet you in the bread and wine.
     We meet you in each other.

11   Morning by morning you waken us
         to hear your word.
     Your Son speaks to us.
     Your Spirit comes to us.
     Kindling in us hopes
         we did not know we had.
     Dreams we never knew we possessed.
     Your Spirit makes us a people, Lord.
     Your people, united by your Spirit.
     Speak to us, Lord,
         in the bread's breaking,
         and in each other.

12   Your love is sufficient, Lord,
         for all our needs.
     We gather up your manna daily,
         enough for this day,
         enough for this hour,
         but no more.
     Tomorrow we will see your love again,
         fresh for our new needs.
     Dear Lord, you come to us daily.

13   Heal us, cleanse us, mend us.
     Bind our fractured parts together
         in your unity, your peace.
     Come to us, Lord,
         come to us now,
         as a garden ready to be watered,
         your servants are waiting.

14   We recall your Son's death and resurrection,
            his death on the cross,
            his brief life on earth,
            for our sakes.
        We tell forth his resurrection in us.

The Prayer of Consecration and the Communion

That same day two of them were on their way to a village called Emmaus, about seven miles from Jerusalem . . . As they talked with one another Jesus himself came up and walked beside them, but something held their eyes from knowing who it was . . . And when they had sat down at the table, he took the bread and blessed it . . .
Luke 24

It is never easy to pinpoint the exact moment in any celebration of the sacrament when Jesus himself starts to walk beside us, and the congregation of two, or a hundred and two, is increased by one.

Jesus is always walking beside us, though we may not feel conscious of his presence, or realise till much later those people or apparently trivial moments through which he spoke.

Most celebrations end with our going back the way we have come, to lives and people that may appear exactly the same as when we left home. Yet they are not quite the same. For we can tell them 'we have seen the Lord'.

If not with our lips then in our lives, we will give him glory.

'Preach the gospel to every creature, use words if necessary.' (St Francis of Assisi)

ELEMENTS FOR A FIRST PRAYER OF CONSECRATION

Celebrant   My brothers and sisters,
          let us celebrate together
          the mystery of Christ.

People   His coming to earth,
          his life and death for all our sakes,
          his coming again to save us.

All   Our Father who art in heaven,
          may your name be holy.

Celebrant   On the same night he was betrayed
          he took the bread
          and gave you thanks.

People   We are your people, Lord,
          waiting to be fed.

Celebrant   He broke the bread
          and gave it to his disciples.

People   We are your disciples, Lord.
          With these few loaves
          a nation will be nourished.
          With this life offered
          the world itself is blessed.

All   May your kingdom come.
          May your will be done as in heaven,
          so on earth.

Celebrant   In the same way he took the cup.

People   We are the branches, Lord,
          nourished on your vine.

Celebrant   He gave it to his disciples saying,
        'This is my blood,
        shed for you and for many,
        for sins' forgiveness.'

People   Pour out your Spirit, Lord.
        Your cup is never empty.
        We drink this wine for our forgiveness,
          and the world's.
        We do this in remembrance of you.

All   We show forth your life again.
        We give you glory.

Elements for a Second Prayer of Consecration

Celebrant   We offer to you, Lord,
   that which pleases you most.
A life of love,
   expressed in a lonely birth.
A life of love,
   expressed in a lonely death
   for all our sakes,
   each of us offering ourselves
   for others.
We offer you ourselves,
   in union with your Son Jesus.
We show forth his life and death,
   until he comes again.
Even so, Lord Jesus,
   come quickly.

All   Christ has died.
Christ is risen.
Christ will come again.

Celebrant   On the same night he was betrayed
   he took the bread
   and gave you thanks.

People   He broke it for our sakes,
   and gave it that we might eat,
   be comforted,
   and raised to life.

Celebrant   He took the cup and blessed it.
This cup of the new covenant,
   this life poured out for others
   to the very end.

People   And yet his cup
   is always full,
   and runs over with
   his love for us.

All   This is your body, Lord,
        given for us.
        This is your life's blood,
        poured out for all our sakes.

Celebrant   We offer ourselves to you, Father,
            in union with your Son Jesus.
            We pray for the peace of the whole world.
            We receive your life into our own.
            Your love receives us.
            We offer all that we are to you.
            Our sins for your forgiveness.
            Our weakness for your strength.
            Our lives for your service,
                now and always.

All   Mary, pray for us.
        Joseph, protect us.
        With all your saints, dear Lord,
            living and departed,
            we give you glory.

ELEMENTS FOR A THIRD PRAYER OF CONSECRATION

All
Dear Lord,
we come before you
with bread and wine.
Tokens of your love for us,
sustaining us daily.
We meet in the name of your Son Jesus.

Celebrant
On the same night he was betrayed
he took the bread and blessed it.
He broke it saying,
'This is my body given for you.
Do this in remembrance of me.'

People
So may we give our lives, Lord,
to be blessed and broken in your service,
each of us for the other.

Celebrant
In the same way he took the cup,
and poured out his life for us
to the very end.

People
The cup of your love is never empty, Lord.
It runs over with your goodness.

All
So may our lives be poured out, Lord,
and offered to the very end.
We cannot give what we have not first received.
Give us your life now, Lord.
Come to us, refresh us.
Fill every part of us with praise.

Celebrant
With this bread and with this cup
we show forth his life again,
and receive our own.
We proclaim his birth in Bethlehem,
his life and death for all our sakes.
We proclaim his resurrection
and our own.

All   Even so Lord Jesus,
           come quickly.

The Lord's Prayer

All   Christ has died.
           Christ is risen.
           Christ will come again.

Celebrant   We remember at this communion
           all souls living and departed,
           the whole company of Christ's Church,
           God's chosen people, the Jews.

People   All those you have chosen, Lord,
           all those who have chosen you.

Celebrant   We pray for all those who suffer:
           the poor,
           the bereaved,
           the homeless,
           those without hope.

People   Give them your hope, Lord.
           Come to them speedily.
           Come to us now.
           Give us all your peace.
           This is your world, Lord.
           Save us now.

ADDITIONAL PRAYERS FOR THE CONSECRATION

1   Lord, accept this Mass we offer.
When we are poor and neglected,
   and all the doors of society are closed against us,
   you come to us in our stable.
You find us a home,
   you send your shepherds to call us by name,
   keep watch over us.
Your wise men arrive,
   our living will not be in vain.
To earth's farthest bounds
   will the effects of our lives be felt.
You give us your gifts.
Lonely on our cross,
   you come to us.
Broken in our grave,
   you roll back the stone,
   declare we are alive.
Lord, we offer this Mass to you,
   in union with your Son Jesus.
We are broken and alone,
   but your Spirit sustains us
   and lifts us up.
We offer you our lives,
   we are risen with Christ,
   we live to your glory.

2   As often as we break this bread,
   we show your life again.
As often as we drink this cup,
   we show your death and resurrection.
Your Son's death is our life, Lord,
   his resurrection is our own.
Sunday by Sunday
   we come to the tomb
   and see no sign of death,
   only of love's triumph,
   and our own calling and renewal.

3   We do this in remembrance of you, Lord,
            who brought your people out of slavery,
            who bring us out of bondage and servitude,
            out of darkness into light,
            out of sin and dereliction
            to serve you in glory.
        You are our friend, Lord.
        Father before us,
            Son beside us,
            Spirit within us.
        You never leave us.
        You bring us to your kingdom.

4   We meet in your Son's name,
            beneath the shadow of his cross.
        To the world it was defeat,
            to us it is victory.
        To the world failure,
            to us, the triumph of your love.
        We proclaim this life, Lord,
            we set it forth
            in bread and wine.
        A meal for all your children,
            each of us welcomed at your table.

5   This is your body, Lord,
            this people here,
            met in your name,
            eating the bread of your new covenant,
            love's kingdom on earth established.
        This is your blood, Lord,
            this is your life,
            flowing in our veins,
            one for another,
            this life poured out
            for all of us,
            to heal us, renew us,
            bring us new life.

6   This is your body, Lord,
         this bread we share.
     This is your life, your blood
         shed for us, given for us,
         this cup we drink.
     We are your body, Lord,
         alive by your grace,
         your Spirit only
         enlivens us,
         gives us your peace.

7   Take the cup now, Lord.
     Take it again.
     Bless it.
     Turn the water of our lives into wine.
     Turn the wine of our suffering
         into life for the world.
     Come to us now, Lord.
     Your people are waiting.

8   This is your body, Lord,
         but also our own.
     Our own lives broken,
         offered in your service,
         shared with each other.
     This is your cup, Lord,
         but also our own.
     Your blood flows in our veins,
         assists us, gives us life.
     We cannot drink your cup, Lord,
         you drank that for us years ago.
     And yet we do drink your cup,
         and make your life our own,
         each of us for the other.

9
Our hearts are open to your word, Lord.
You know our need of you before we ask.
Our weaknesses before we confess them,
Our failures in your word,
  our doors so firmly fastened
  against your love.
Come to us now, Lord
  heal us, save us.
We are your servants,
  your vessels,
  waiting to be filled.

10
We recall Jesus' death, Lord,
  the night he was betrayed.
He took bread and blessed it
  that we might eat.
Took wine and poured it,
  that we might receive his life.
This is his body, given for us.
This is his blood, for all his people shed.
We recall your Son's death, dear Father.
We receive his resurrection
  but also our own.

11
We offer you this bread and wine.
Is it not the body of your Son?
His life for us,
  your love for us in him.
Are we not his body, his people also?
This wine we drink,
  is it not his life, your life,
  flowing in our veins?
We drink it to your glory.

12   There is no holy communion, Lord,
         without holy community.
     Help us to belong to your family first.
     Your ancient people, the Jews,
         renewed and refreshed by the life and death
         of your servant Jesus.
     In him, we are all renewed.
     By your Spirit, we all share his resurrection.
     Help us to tell forth your story, Lord,
         to all peoples in all lands.
     Beginning here,
         beginning now.

13   We proclaim the life of your Son, Lord,
         here at this table
         as his life demands of us.
     The bread set out,
         that all may feed.
     The cup of affliction,
         but also joy,
             from which we drink.
     We offer our lives to you, Lord,
         in union with his own.
     Christ in us,
         Messiah in each one of us.
     Your love for each of us continuously.

14   Set us up upon the rock
         that is higher than we are.
     You are our rock, Lord,
         we build our lives on you.
     Without you, we can do nothing.
     By your grace, we can do everything.
     There is no limit,
         to your grace in our own lives.
     Come to us now, Lord.
     Cleanse us, refresh us, help us.
     Assist us by your grace to start again.

15
    We meet in your name, Lord,
      but also in our own.
    You give us our name, Lord,
      in the waters of baptism,
      in the water of our tears,
      as we repent,
      turn back toward you daily.
    Love is your name, Lord,
      sacrifice for us is your meaning.
    We offer our own lives also,
      in this bread and in this wine,
      each of us given for the other.

16
    We show forth your death, Lord.
    To the world it is defeat
      but to us victory.
    To the world it is a life's ending,
      to us resurrection.
    To the world failure,
      to us love and victory beyond comparison.
    We show forth your death, Lord.
    We proclaim our own resurrection.

17
    Where there is hatred, Lord,
      let us sow love.
    Where there is injury,
      pardon.
    Where there is despair,
      hope.
    Here at this table, Lord,
      to which your love invites us,
      we set forth and proclaim
      the life of your Son.
    Where there is war,
      let there be peace,
      through this life
      which we together
      proclaim and share.

18

We break this bread, Lord,
   to share it with each other.
Your Son's life given freely
   to each one of us.
When we are blind,
   you help us to see.
When we are deaf
   to love's entreaties,
   you speak to us.
When we are dumb,
   you touch our lips
   to sing your praises,
   communicate your love.

19

We drink to your health, Lord,
   but also to our own.
And to the world's salvation.
We eat this bread of affliction
   but also life.
Food to sustain us
   in our wanderings
   and in our uncertainty.
We offer you our lives,
   in union with your Son Jesus.
We proclaim his life to all the world
   but in your love
   and in your name first of all.

The Gloria

. . . and suddenly there was with the Angel a multitude of the heavenly host praising God and saying 'Glory to God in the highest and on earth peace, good will to his people on earth' . . .
Luke 2:13-14

None of us can be thinking or praying all the time. We would get exhausted. There is a place for praising only, and giving glory: and resting in God or life, rather than asking things of it. There is a place for listening to some-one else's song and joining in a tune we did not have to labour to compose. And yet the tune belongs to us also. We are all part of God's symphony. The note or notes sounded by our lives are each one quite distinctive. 'The Lord loves to hear his crows as well as his nightingales.'

1
Glory be to God on high,
   and on the earth his peace.
With angels and archangels
   we praise his holy name.
With shepherds in the field,
   blinded by the light of God's love,
   we kneel and adore him.

2
Glory to you, Lord,
   in the morning and in the evening.
Glory to you, when we are young.
Glory, when we are old.
All the stages of our life give you glory.
All the stages of this day.
In the morning and in the evening,
   we praise your holy name.

3
We recall your Son's death, Lord.
We show it forth proudly.
We proclaim it.
That to die in poverty,
    condemned by all the world,
    this is true wealth.
That to die alone,
    everyone neglecting you,
    no one understanding,
    this is true company.
That to die forgiving, speaking kindly
    to those who handed you over,
    this is true life.
And the world's renewal.

4
Dear Lord, we praise you.
With bread that human hands have made
    to give us life.
And give you glory.
With wine that human hands have poured,
    grapes of your vine,
    pressed down and running over.
Our cup is full, Lord,
    to overflowing,
    with all your goodness for us.
In the life of your Son Jesus,
    we give you glory.

5
You make the morning and the night, Lord.
One follows the other,
    each in its proper place
    give you glory.
The night for sleeping,
    secure in your love.
The day for service,
    as well as we may.
Each in our own place
    we give you glory.

6   We give you glory, Lord,
        as the first shepherds did
        who celebrated your birth,
        kept watch over you.
    We give you glory, Lord,
        for your care of us,
        your watching over
        our souls' needs day by day.
    We give you glory for our lives also.
    In our own lives
        and in our deaths we praise you.
    In your own life,
        and in your Son's death,
        we find resurrection.

THE REDEDICATION OF OURSELVES

1   We trust in you, Lord,
        but also in ourselves.
    What you have done in us,
        what you will do.
    Your plans for us are good, Lord.
    For love's purpose only
        are we formed,
        to serve you,
        to serve others in you,
        to be loved by you for ever.

2   We are your people, Lord,
        you have chosen us.
    By the sea of Galilee
        we heard your word.
    When we were in our own homes,
        you saw us and called us.
    When we worked at our fishing nets,
        or counted the gifts you had given us,
        you spoke to us saying
        love is the greatest gift of all.

3   Come, Lord, in this communion.
    Come, Lord, in this community.
    We are a people, first of all.
    Your people, even when
        two or three are present.
    We are your people,
        met in your name,
        called by your Spirit,
        waiting for instruction.
    Dear Lord,
        we praise you.

4   Help us to hear the meaning of your life, Lord.
    Your love for us,
        your care for all your children.
    It is better to be born in ignominy,
        than to leave others outside
        to live in the stable.
    It is better to preach your word
        than to ignore its kindness,
        better to die in desolation
        than curse those who hate us.
    Better to rise again on the third day
        in love's name, and no one else's.
    Dear Lord, we give you glory.

5   Let us be glad and rejoice in your friendship, Lord.
    You who have made us,
        and brought us safely to this day.
    Through trials and tribulations
        you support us,
        you never leave us,
        however far we wander
        from your word, your ways.
    Come to us now, Lord,
    Bless us, refresh us, revive us.
    We rejoice in your friendship,
        and in our own.

6

We hold up our hands to you in prayer,
   we hold up our lives.
The fingers and hands
   your love has lent us.
The five loaves and two fishes
   your love has given us,
   with which to praise you
   and feed the world.
We hold up our lives to you, Lord,
   we wait for your blessing.
In your time and by your Spirit
   may the world be fed.

7

We are your people, Lord.
Bread baked by your mother's hand,
   kneaded and made ready
   to feed a hungry world.
We are your vineyard, Lord.
You are the gardener.
We are the vine,
   each one of us a branch,
   nourished by your love,
   your dying for us daily.
You are the vine.
We are the branches.
Each of us in our own way,
   grows to your glory.

8

We drink your cup, Lord,
   your life flows in our veins.
We eat this bread
   of your affliction
   and our own.
For forty years your people travelled,
   seeking rest.
You bring us to the kingdom, Lord,
   we enter Jerusalem.
This is the promised land.

9
    We pray for your Church, Lord,
       near and far,
       here and now,
       for our own lives also.
    For the peace of the whole world,
       for your peace
       in our own country.
    For those who suffer
       in body, mind or spirit,
       through hunger, thirst or loneliness,
       who suffer oppression.
    You have made of one blood
       all nations of the earth
       to live in harmony.
    Living and departed.
    Lord, we praise you,
       we adore you.

10
    We believe in your Church, Lord.
    Despite all our sins,
       you inhabit us,
       influence us,
       bring us to our journey's end.
    The boat launched at Galilee
       is still travelling,
       still at work.
    There is room in her for all your children.
    Each of us has our own place,
       beside the lobster pots
       and Peter and Andrew's fishing tackle.
    It is your Church, Lord,
       though the waves are rough.
    You speak to us through her.
    Your Spirit inspires us
       and leads us forward.

11 We are not saved by words, Lord,
        but by your word.
    This life spoken,
        this life offered for us,
        by us daily.
    Not only in the bread and wine,
        but in our own lives
        laid down for your sake,
        by your grace,
        for each other.
    We reach out to the whole world, Lord,
        and to you
        in your Son's life first of all.

12 Free us from slavery, Lord,
        the world's cruelty,
        our own dominion over each other.
    You bring us out of slavery.
    Those chains which we fasten daily,
        your Spirit loosens.
    You bring us to Jerusalem,
        here and now
        we enter the city of peace.
    We enter by your word
        the land your love has promised,
        your sacrifice still makes possible.

Departing

Not for these alone do I pray, but for those who will believe through them.
from John 17:20

When Jesus first fed five thousand people with the five loaves and two small fishes, all that life had given him, he asked his disciples to gather up the fragments that remained, so that nothing would be lost. We have been doing it ever since.

Only so many people can come to any particular celebration. But when we go out of God's house we do not go out of his presence. All the people we meet are members of his family, if not immediately of ours. We pray for them, and wish them well. That they may be blessed and fed by God's love also.

Not for us alone does Jesus pray. But for those who will believe, through us.

Celebrant   We have come into your house, Lord.

People   We are your house,
         we are the household of your faith.

Celebrant   We have come into your presence, Lord.

People   We are in your presence daily,
         we love you, we serve you,
         we give you praise.

Celebrant   We have met around your table, Lord.

People   Your table is our table,
         your bread and wine,
         our own flesh and blood.
      Dear Lord, we praise you daily.

1
Defend us, Lord.
You are our shield,
   the rock on which we build,
   our shelter in the storm.
We rest in your word.
We rest in each other.
We go out in the power of your Spirit,
   to love you and serve you.

2
Let nothing be lost, Lord,
   gather up the fragments that remain,
   of this feast, of our own lives.
Nothing is ever wasted, Lord,
   those things we have forgotten,
   those people who have passed through
   our lives.
We offer ourselves to you, Lord,
   our future is safe in your hands.
We love you and serve you today.

3
We will do great things through you, Lord.
Greater than you did,
   because you are with us.
More than you did,
   for you were one and we are many.
Yet you are many in us, Lord,
   through us.
Your work is our work,
   your life is ours,
   now and for ever.

4
We are your body, Lord,
   nourished by your feast.
We love you, we serve you.

5   To you be the glory, Lord,
        in our own lives.
    To you be the power,
        for you are our strength.
    To you be our prayer,
        for you are our love,
        our hope, our stay.

6   We pray for your Church, Lord,
        in all lands and in all places.
    We are your Church, Lord,
        ready to serve you.
    We pray for your Church, Lord,
        all ages in a moment of time,
        our friends departed
        in your love and care.
    They are safe, Lord,
        they join their praises to ours.
    They encourage us, pray for us.
    Mary and Joseph, your servants,
        pray for us daily.

7   We set our hope on you, Lord.
    You are our strength, and our song.
    You are the story that we tell,
        day by day.
    You are our friend in the past,
        love recorded,
        love told again daily.
    You are our hope in the future,
        no one else knowing,
        no one else caring,
        as you do.
    You are our hope and strength
        today and always.

8   You are the well of our life, Lord.
     A deep well, filled with water.
     Of your love for us,
         there is no end.
     The more we drink from your cup,
         the more there is to drink.
     Like life-giving waters,
         you refresh us and cleanse us,
         and feed us.
     It is a new day, a new beginning.

9   You are our strength, Lord,
         our life and our song.
     Daily we speak of your goodness
         your loving kindness
         to all your children.
     We tell your story,
         day by day we tell of your goodness.
     With our lips and with our lives
         we serve and obey you.

10   We believe in you, Lord,
         but also in ourselves.
     We are your servants, Lord,
         waiting on your word.
     Your breath in our lungs,
         your life in our hearts.
     One by one we serve you,
         each in our own way,
         we give you glory.
     We lose ourselves in your love for us.
     We lose ourselves but find ourselves,
         in this community
         which gives you praise.

11   We do not look for your second coming, Lord,
          we are content with your first.
      Here and now you save us,
          come to us,
          bless us,
          sustain us.
      Give us strength when we are weary,
          enable us to rest in your love,
          enable us to run
          in the way of love's command.
      Even so, Lord Jesus, come quickly.

12   We ask you to do more in our lives, Lord,
          that we may do less.
      Relying on your friendship for us,
          your words of encouragement,
          spoken daily,
          dwelt on at leisure.
      We feed on your word, Lord.
      We feed on the life of your Son,
          expressed in this fellowship,
          each one of us praying for the other.

13   You do not give us what we deserve, Lord,
          but what we need.
      Your love, your kindness,
          your understanding, your forgiveness.
      Out of nothing you create us daily.
      Each moment is the gift of your love,
          the world preventing you,
          the world getting in your way.
      Our hearts are fixed on you only, Lord.
      You who love us unreservedly.

14   Dear Lord, hear my prayer.
Though I am born in a stable,
  and all the doors of society
  are closed against me,
  you send me your shepherds
  to watch over me,
  and call me by name.
Wise men from the east arrive,
  at your bidding alone,
  to say that my obscure birth
  will yet influence and affect
  all the world.
And though I die in loneliness,
  no one understanding,
  and am buried in another's tomb
  with no prayers said
  to speed my journey.
Yet will you send your messengers
  to roll back the stone
  and call me back, saying to the world:
  I am alive for ever.

15   Our spirits rise to greet you, Lord.
We wait on your word.
Like birds in the sky,
  we rest on your wind.
Like fishes in the sea,
  we swim in the ocean of your love.
Our lives are limited
  to this time and place.
Your love for us is limitless.
Like the stars in the sky,
  and the sand on the sea shore,
  so shall the opportunities of this day
  afford you glory.

16   Do not hide your face from us, Lord.
Show us your love,
    but also your purposes.
Give us your peace,
    but also your work to do,
    our own duties to perform.
Give us your love, Lord,
    that we may give to others,
    love others,
    for your Son's sake only.

17   May your name be kept holy, Lord.
Your meaning for us, in the world.
Your love for the world,
    which never changes.
For if we remain true to your name, Lord,
    your kingdom will come.
And where your kingdom is,
    there may our hearts be always.

18   Not only with our lips but with our life,
    here in this place,
    one with another,
    your whole Church is present,
    praying and believing.
Living and departed,
    young and old,
    each of us contributing
    our own part to your praises.
Not only with our lips
    but with our lives,
    we will serve you.

19   Not only with our lips, Lord,
          but with our lives,
          we will praise you.
      Not only with this bread and wine,
          not only with these prayers and hymns,
          but all our lives in every part
          tell out your story.

20   Do not leave us, Lord,
          when we are old and grey-headed.
      Come to us in your strength,
          though we are weaker.
      Come to us in your power.
      Make us strong
          in the memory of your kindness.
      May our hearts be deep
          because of our sins forgiven,
          and friends retained.
      Nothing is lost, Lord.
          We are safe in your hands for ever.

Evening Prayers

1
       We praise you in the evening of our lives,
          when the nets we have let down
          at your command,
          into your sea,
          have taken nothing.
       We praise you in the desert places,
          when we have nothing to eat,
          and day is nearly over.
       We praise you when the oil in our lamp
          runs low,
          and there is no replacement,
          no refilling.
       We praise you in the darkness, Lord,
          and await your morning.

2
       The night comes, Lord,
          when no one can work.
       Nor should we need to,
          when the day is over,
          and we return ourselves to you,
          our work to you,
          the world to you,
          ourselves to your love and keeping.
       Help us to rest in your word, Lord.
       Keep our minds safe from all worries,
          especially those that will not go away.
       Help us to sleep until morning.

3
       Ponder my words, Lord.
       Listen to them closely.
       As we listen to yours.
       We who are too shy to speak,
          uncertain how to praise you.
       Yet we do praise you.
       Your love requests it.
       We praise you as the sun goes down.

A Prayer for Pentecost

Today is Pentecost, Lord.
Your people are renewed
  and created again,
  by the coming of your Spirit.
Come to us again, Lord,
  enable us to praise you
  with many voices,
  each one our own.
But help us to proclaim your love
  with one heart,
  one mind,
  one voice,
  in a language everyone can understand.

A Prayer for Christmas

It is Christmas, Lord,
  and we do not celebrate
  your Son's birth only:
  but every son,
  every daughter.
While the Emperor counts everybody
  in his empire,
  you count us your friends.
While the Emperor proclaims:
  count everybody,
  your love announces:
  everybody counts.